WONDERFUL
World

NICOLA BAXTER

PRINCETON ■ LONDON

How to Use This Book

Cross-references

Above some of the chapter titles, you will find a list of other chapters in the book that are related to the topic. Turn to these pages to find out more about each subject.

See for yourself

See-for-yourself bubbles give you the chance to test out some of the ideas in this book. They explain what you will need and what you have to do to see if an idea really works.

Quiz corner

In the quiz corner, you will find a list of questions. The answers to the quiz questions are somewhere in the same chapter. Try to answer all the questions about each subject.

Chatterboxes

Chatterboxes give you interesting facts about other things that are related to the subject.

Glossary

Difficult words are explained in the glossary on page 31. These words are in **bold** type in the book. Look them up in the glossary to find out what they mean.

Index

The index is on page 32. It is a list of important words mentioned in the book, with page numbers next to the entries. If you want to read about a subject, look it up in the index, then turn to the page number given.

Contents

Planet Earth

Our **planet** Earth is never still. It is moving and changing all the time. We cannot feel it, but our planet is spinning in space. It is not floating freely but follows a set path around the nearest star, which is the sun. In turn, a smaller mass, the moon, moves steadily around Earth.

The Earth
Earth travels around, or **orbits**, the sun in just over 365 days, which is one year. While Earth is orbiting the sun, it spins like a top. It makes one complete spin every twenty-four hours.

The moon's path around Earth ....

Earth ....

moon ....

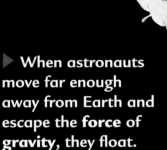

▶ When astronauts move far enough away from Earth and escape the **force** of **gravity**, they float.

Gravity
Earth and the sun pull things toward them with a force called gravity. Gravity keeps everything, including people, trees, rocks and water, pulled down onto Earth's surface. Without gravity, everything would float off into space.

The moon
The moon travels around Earth once every four weeks. On its way, it seems to change shape, from a circle to a thin curve, or crescent. This is because the sun lights up different parts of the moon as it makes its journey.

.....sun

Quiz Corner

- How long does Earth take to travel around the sun?
- What is the name of the force that keeps us from floating off into space?
- Does Earth move around the moon?
- Why does it get dark at night?

The sun
The sun is really a huge ball of fire. All Earth's heat and light come from the Sun. Living things cannot survive without it.

Earth's path around the sun

sun..........

The sun and Earth
The hottest part of Earth is around its middle. We draw an imaginary line here and call it the **equator**.

When your part of the Earth is turned toward the sun, it is day. When it is turned away, it is night.

Earth.............

equator.......

night   day   sun's rays

look at: Volcanoes, page 8; Earthquakes, page 10

Inside Earth

Earth is made up of layers. Beneath the top layers are metals and rocks that are so hot they have melted, or are molten. The top layers can tell us what Earth was like millions of years ago. These layers are changing all the time.

The crust is made up of rocks and soil. This layer and the top part of the mantle float on the molten layer below.

The mantle is under the crust. It is made of rock that is so hot that parts of it are slowly moving.

The outer core is made of molten metals, most of which is iron.

mantle

outer core

inner core

crust

The moving Earth
Millions of years ago, all the land on Earth was one huge **continent**. Gradually the land moved apart. It is still moving very slowly.

the world today

millions of years ago

The inner core is a solid ball of metal which is extremely hot.

6

The secrets of rock

Beneath the soil, there is solid rock, which in some places pokes above ground. Millions of years ago, some of this rock was molten and flowed over the ground. Then it slowly cooled. Above the rock, there is a layer of subsoil.

▶ Earth's crust is made up of layers. The layer we know best, called soil, is home to many living things.

Fossils

Sometimes, when rocks are forming, the body of a plant or animal is trapped between the layers. When the body rots away, it leaves a space. This space slowly fills up with rock, making a copy of the body, called a **fossil**.

▶ The fossilized shell of an **extinct** creature called an ammonite looks like a snail.

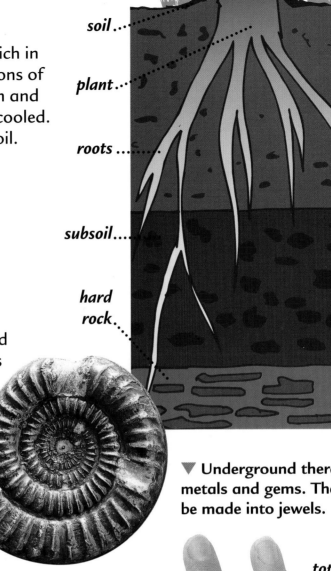

soil

plant

roots

subsoil

hard rock

▼ Underground there are metals and gems. These can be made into jewels.

Quiz Corner

● What is the top layer of Earth called?

● What is the name of a rock that has the shape of the body of a living thing from long ago?

● How many continents were there millions of years ago?

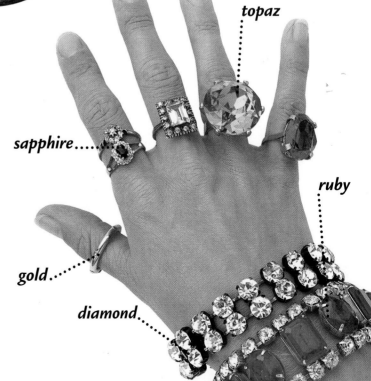

topaz

sapphire

ruby

gold

diamond

look at: Inside Earth, page 6; Mountains, page 14

Volcanoes

A volcano is a mountain that has gases and hot liquid rock, called **magma**, inside it. When **pressure** builds up inside the volcano, the gases and magma erupt, or explode, from the top as lava. An **extinct** volcano will never erupt again, but an active volcano may be quiet for many years, then suddenly erupt.

▼ Japanese macaque monkeys enjoy bathing in hot springs.

Inside a volcano
Over many years, a volcano is built up from layers of ash and **molten** lava that flow down from the opening, or vent. The ash and lava cool and become rock. This is why many volcanoes are cone-shaped.

vent ········· lava

············· magma

Geysers and hot springs
Sometimes underground lakes and rivers pass over magma. When this happens, water is heated under **pressure** and may suddenly spurt up in a hot fountain, called a geyser, or bubble up into hot springs.

SEE FOR YOURSELF

You can see what happens when gases are put under pressure by shaking a plastic bottle half full of seltzer water. Be very careful as you take the top off, because the liquid inside acts just like the lava in a volcano!

▼ Volcanoes throw out dust and ash as well as molten lava. It is difficult for plants and animals to live on the slopes of active volcanoes.

Quiz Corner

- What is the hot, liquid rock inside a volcano called?

- What happens when rivers pass over magma?

- Why don't many plants and animals live on active volcanoes?

- What shape are most volcanoes?

look at: Inside Earth, page 6

Earthquakes

Earthquakes happen when rocks along cracks in Earth's **crust** move. This can make the crust shake and break. The shaking may be so slight that you can hardly feel it, or it may cause buildings to fall to the ground. When earthquakes happen under the sea, they sometimes make enormous waves called tsunami.

▲ This house, shaken by an earthquake, has become unsafe.

Fault lines
Usually, earthquakes happen at places where there are breaks in Earth's crust, called faults. Most parts of Earth do not have earthquakes.

▲ The San Andreas fault in California can be seen clearly from the air.

CHATTERBOX

Animals often warn people that an earthquake is coming. Usually quiet animals become restless. Geese honk noisily and other birds fly around in circles.

Standing firm

To make sure that a building will stay standing during an earthquake, builders put metal rods inside concrete building blocks. They also leave enough space for the walls of the building to move a little. This allows even tall skyscrapers to be built in areas where earthquakes may occur.

▶ **The modern Transamerica Pyramid Building in San Francisco was built to remain standing during an earthquake.**

Measuring earthquakes

Scientists use the Richter scale and the Mercalli scale to measure the size of an earthquake. The Mercalli scale describes what happens during an earthquake.

 On the Mercalli scale at scale 4, windows, pots and pans rattle.

 At scale 6, furniture moves, windows break and cracks appear in walls.

 At scale 8, bridges and chimneys may fall. Buildings move on their foundations.

 At scale 10, most buildings cannot stand. Many trees fall down.

Quiz Corner

- What are broken places in Earth's crust called?
- What is the name of the scale scientists use to describe what happens during an earthquake?
- What can happen when there is an earthquake under the sea?

look at: Rivers and Lakes, page 16

Land Shapes

The shape of the land is changing all the time. Natural **forces**, including wind, water and ice, can wear away rocks, mountains and soil. This is called **erosion**. These changes happen gradually, over many years.

Caves
Rainwater and underground rivers can **erode** rocks, forming caves. These become homes for bats and birds. When water drips from the roof of a cave, **chemicals** in the water can make long rock shapes grow from the ceiling. These are called stalactites. Similar shapes standing on the floor are called stalagmites.

Land shaped by water
When water rushes through rocks, it carves out a path for itself. Over millions of years, this path can become a deep **valley**. The Grand Canyon was made by the Colorado River, which cut through rocks that are up to two billion years old. The Grand Canyon is 275 miles long and over one mile deep.

▲ Over millions of years, Antelope Canyon in Arizona was formed by water carving a path through pink sandstone rock.

Ice ages

Several times in the past, large parts of Earth were covered with ice. When huge sheets of the ice, called **glaciers,** moved, they pushed rocks and soil in front of them, making valleys and hills.

▼ There are still glaciers today, moving slowly and changing the landscape gradually.

▲ Long ago, rivers carved out strange-shaped hills in Monument Valley, in Utah and Arizona. Today the land is desert, but windblown sand still erodes the rocks.

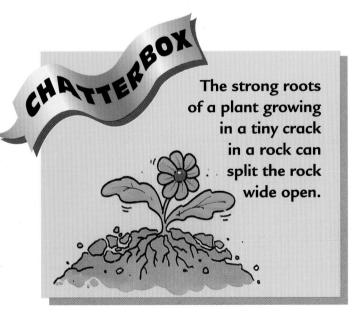

CHATTERBOX

The strong roots of a plant growing in a tiny crack in a rock can split the rock wide open.

Quiz Corner

● What is the long rock shape hanging from the roof of a cave called?

● Which river made the Grand Canyon?

● What is a huge sheet of ice on land called?

● Which part of a plant can split a rock?

look at: Inside Earth, page 6; Volcanoes, page 8

Mountains

Mountain ranges are strips of high land. They have been made over millions of years and they continue to change. In some places, mountains were formed where one part of Earth's **crust** pushed against another part, making huge folds of rock. In other places, Earth's crust broke into large pieces, which moved up or down to make new mountains.

▼ The longest mountain range in the world is the Andes, which runs down the western side of the **continent** of South America.

SEE FOR YOURSELF

Roll out three thick layers of modelling clay and place them one on top of the other. Cut through the layers to make a strip about 8 inches long. Push the ends of the strip until the middle rises and folds. The colored layers show the shapes of the rocks inside "fold" mountains.

The highest mountains
The Himalayan mountain range, in central Asia, is the highest in the world. The range was formed when parts of the crust pushed against each other, squeezing up the rock.

14

Cold on top

Toward the top of a mountain, the **temperature** drops. This means that even in hot parts of the world, mountain tops are covered with ice and snow. Few plants and animals can survive on the cold higher mountain slopes. Plants grow low to the ground to avoid the icy winds.

 Llamas are one of the most useful animals to the mountain peoples of South America. They can carry heavy loads along the mountain paths, and their thick wool can be made into warm clothes.

Quiz Corner

● What is a strip of high land called?

● Where are the highest mountains in the world?

● What is the longest mountain range in the world?

● Which animal is important to the mountain peoples of South America?

look at: Mountains, page 14; Oceans, page 18

Rivers and Lakes

The beginning, or source, of a river is often a mountain spring. Water flows down the mountain, carving out the easiest path to the sea. It carries soil and even rocks with it. Large areas of water, or lakes, occur when rainwater gathers in the top of volcanoes, or where glaciers melt. They can also be man-made.

CHATTERBOX

Some people say they have seen a monster in a lake called Loch Ness in Scotland. The loch is extremely deep, so it is difficult to prove whether the monster, called Nessie, exists or not.

▲ Lake Atitlan, in Guatemala, is a good source of fish for food. The lake, with a dam of volcanic ash, fills an ancient valley.

Waterfalls
When water tumbles over a huge step of rock, it makes a waterfall. The water flows over hard rock and **erodes** soft rock below. Sometimes the soft rock is so eroded, the hard rock at the top of the waterfall hangs forward.

▲ The Iguazu Falls form part of the border between Brazil and Argentina in South America.

▶ Big rocks in rivers make water splash and swirl into white water. Many people enjoy paddling rafts over this fast-flowing water.

Oxbow lakes
An oxbow lake is made when the path of a river changes course. A big bend in a river can become a lake if the river then flows straight, leaving its bend cut off by a bank of soil.

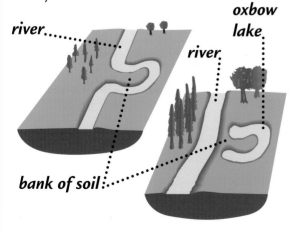

river

oxbow lake

river

bank of soil

Quiz Corner
- In what country is Loch Ness located?
- What shape is an oxbow lake?
- What makes river water swirl into white water?
- How are lakes created?

look at: Mountains, page 14; Rivers and Lakes, page 16

Oceans

Most of our **planet** is covered by water, not by land. Four large oceans and many smaller seas cover over half of Earth. These oceans and seas are not still. The water flows forwards and backwards in movements called **tides**. At high tide, the water moves farther onto the land. At low tide, it falls back again. The wind also moves the water into waves, which rise up and fall down.

Undersea ups and downs

There are mountains and **valleys** under the sea, just as there are on land. If Mount Everest were placed in the deepest **trench** in the Pacific Ocean, its top would not reach the water's surface.

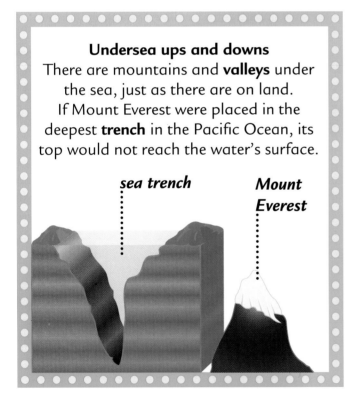

sea trench

Mount Everest

CHATTERBOX

It is easier to float in the sea than in freshwater because seawater is salty. The saltiest sea in the world is the Dead Sea in Israel.

Oceans

The four oceans of the world are the Pacific Ocean, the Atlantic Ocean, the Indian Ocean and the Arctic Ocean. The largest of these is the Pacific Ocean.

► The wind can make huge waves crash onto the beach. Many people enjoy surfing on these waves.

Wind and waves

When the wind blows across the sea, it whips the water into waves. A little breeze can cause ripples, while a gale can make huge waves. Seawater looks as if it is moving along, but it is really moving up and down. It is only where the sea meets the land that waves roll in toward the shore.

▲ Oceans are home to millions of living things. The fish above are looking for food in a coral reef. The foundation of a reef is a rock-like structure made up of the skeletons of tiny sea creatures.

Quiz Corner

● Where is the water at high tide?

● Which is the largest ocean?

● Where is the saltiest sea in the world?

● How much of our planet Earth is covered by oceans and seas?

look at: Land Shapes, page 12; Oceans, page 18

Polar Lands

There are huge areas of snow and ice at the far north and far south of Earth. These are called the North and South Poles. They are the coldest places on Earth.

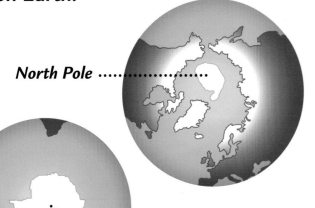

North Pole

South Pole

Iceberg secrets

Sometimes enormous chunks of ice break free from the frozen sea and float away. These icebergs look enormous, but that is only a small part. Nearly all of the ice is under the water.

sea level

Land and sea

At the North Pole, or Arctic, there is no land. The pole lies near the middle of the Arctic Ocean. The top layer of the ocean is frozen into ice and snow, which floats on water. The South Pole, or Antarctic, is land. It is covered by an extremely thick layer of ice.

▶ Icebergs are shaped by the wind and waves.

Arctic seasons

In the Arctic, it is daylight for most of the summer because the sun does not set. In winter, it is nearly always dark because the sun does not rise.

An icebreaker is a ship that cuts paths through ice so that other ships can follow.

CHATTERBOX

The bodies of some animals, such as the hairy mammoths, that lived thousands of years ago, have been found in the polar ice. Just as a freezer keeps food fresh, ice has kept these animals from rotting away.

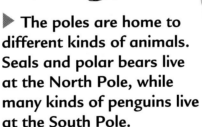

▶ The poles are home to different kinds of animals. Seals and polar bears live at the North Pole, while many kinds of penguins live at the South Pole.

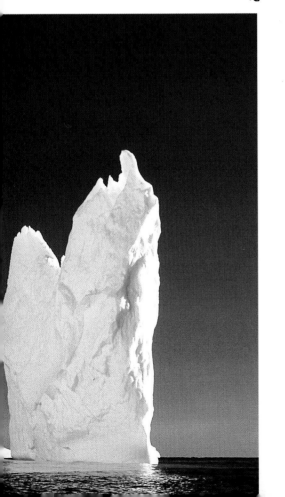

Quiz Corner

- Is most of an iceberg above or below the water?
- What is the area of land at the South Pole called?
- Do polar bears live at the South Pole?
- Is there land at the North Pole?

look at: Land Shapes, page 12

Deserts

Deserts are places where hardly any rain falls and there is almost no water. Living things cannot survive without water, so desert peoples, animals, and plants have to make good use of the little water they can find. Often, deserts are hot, dry places, but they can be cold and dry, too.

The growing desert

Some dry areas have enough rain to grow crops. People and animals can live in these dry places only if it rains every year. Without rain, the land quickly becomes desert. Sometimes, pipes are laid to bring in water from somewhere else.

CHATTERBOX

Desert plants have to work hard to survive. Many store water in their leaves and stems, but they still cannot burst into flower until rain falls. Some desert plants also have prickly thorns to keep animals from eating them.

▼ Dunes are hills of sand that have been shaped by the wind. These crescent-shaped dunes with long tails are called barchans.

▲ Camels carry people and their loads across the desert. A camel can travel a long way without eating and drinking because it stores food and water in its hump.

Cold deserts

The deserts of central Asia are often freezing, especially in winter. Traveling peoples who live in these deserts sleep in tents called yurts.

▼ Yurts are made of tough animal skins and help keep traveling peoples warm and safe at night.

Quiz Corner

● Are all deserts hot?

● How do travelers in central Asian deserts keep warm at night?

● How do desert plants and animals survive ?

● What is a crescent-shaped dune with a long tail called?

look at: Land Shapes, page 12

Grasslands and Wetlands

Grasslands are places where there is enough rain for grass to grow but not enough for many trees to grow. Each continent has its own very large area of grasslands. There are plains, prairies, pampas, steppes and savannas.

Grazing the grasslands

Animals that live on grasslands are always on the move, looking for fresh grass or other animals to eat. Many large animals live on the grasslands. In Africa there are wildebeest and antelope, and in South America there are llamas. Smaller animals also live on grasslands, gnawing at the roots of the grass and burrowing underground.

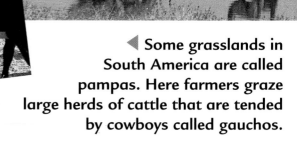

◀ Some grasslands in South America are called pampas. Here farmers graze large herds of cattle that are tended by cowboys called gauchos.

24

Wetlands

The ground in wetlands is usually wet all the time, although it may dry out a little in the summer. There are wetlands in many countries around the world.

▲ Some plants, such as rice, grow best in wetlands. Often, workers gather the rice plants by hand.

▲ Grass grows quickly, especially if it has just rained. In Africa, grazing animals, such as these waterbuck and impala, move slowly over the grasslands, giving the grass behind them time to grow again.

Quiz Corner

● Does rice grow best in dry or wet ground?

● What are some of the grasslands in South America called?

● Why are there few trees in grassland areas?

● Where do wildebeest live?

look at: Land Shapes, page 12; Rivers and Lakes, page 16

Rain Forests

In warm, wet parts of Africa, South America, Asia and Australia, there are huge rain forests. The rain forest floor and towering treetops offer different kinds of homes, or **habitats**, for millions of living things. The trees also give out a gas called **oxygen**, which all living things need to survive.

Rain forest leaves
Many rain forest plants have large leaves that collect water. The leaves of this rubber plant are shaped so that rain will drip off them, fall to the ground and be collected by the roots.

Parts of a rain forest
Thousands of different kinds of plants and animals live in all parts of a rain forest. The bottom part of a rain forest is called the forest floor. The tree trunks and taller plants in the middle make up the understory. The tops of the trees are called the canopy.

▲ The taller trees of this rain forest in Borneo, Asia, reach up into the sunlight. Other plants and animals live on the warm, dark forest floor.

Some of the world's biggest poisonous spiders, called tarantulas, live in the South American rain forests. But really their bite is less poisonous than that of many smaller spiders!

Animal life

Many different animals live in the rain forests of the world, including tigers, porcupines, monkeys, frogs and many different kinds of birds.

Quiz Corner

● Where do tarantulas live?

● Are there any rain forests in Africa?

● Why do many rain forest plants have large leaves?

● Which gas is made by trees and is also in the air we breathe?

▲ In the rain forests of South America, colorful birds fly among the highest branches. A toucan uses its huge beak to pick berries and nuts from the trees.

look at: Deserts, page 22; Grasslands and Wetlands, page 24; Rain Forests, page 26

Taking Care of Earth

Millions of animals and plants have their homes on Earth. Living things, including people, cannot survive by themselves. We all depend on each other. It is up to us to make sure that the way we live does not harm our **planet**. We can do this by saving the Earth's **resources**, or useful things, and being careful to use only what we need.

Recycling

We need Earth's resources to make most of the things we use every day, such as paper, which comes from trees. Instead of throwing things away, we can recycle them, or use them again. This means Earth's resources will not be used as quickly.

▲ Taking care of Earth is something that we can all do. Bottles, cans and paper can be collected and sorted for recycling.

▲ Earth is a beautiful place. Find out more about the area where you live and what people are doing to take care of it.

Energy

Coal, oil and gas are **energy** resources which come from Earth. By using them sensibly, we can help to make sure that there will be resources for people in the future.

SEE FOR YOURSELF

Help take care of Earth by recycling. Save your used cans, bottles and paper and find out where you can take them to be recycled. Check to see whether you can buy recycled items when you go shopping.

Quiz Corner

- How can you help to save Earth's resources?

- What is recycling?

- Name three things that can be recycled.

- From where do coal, gas and oil come?

Amazing Facts

● Earth is getting heavier all the time. Its weight increases by about twenty five tons every day — that's about the same weight as three African elephants. This extra weight is mostly space dust.

☆ *In northern Norway, the sun shines all day and all night for about three months of the year.*

● The longest river in the world is the Nile in Africa. About four thousand miles long, it runs from its source in Burundi to the Mediterranean Sea.

☆ *Did you know that even at night we use sunlight? Moonlight is really the sun's light reflecting off the moon's surface.*

● At the equator, days and nights last exactly the same length of time. They are each twelve hours long.

☆ *The Amazon rain forest in South America is the largest in the world. It is home to more kinds of animals than any other place on Earth. Many more have not yet been discovered.*

● Coal and oil are called fossil fuels. They are a product of the bodies of plants and animals that lived and died millions of years ago.

☆ *Did you know that the Atlantic Ocean is growing? Every year, it grows wider by about two inches, which is about the length of your finger.*

● Nearly ten per cent of the Earth's surface is covered with glaciers all the time. Most of this is the Antarctic ice sheet.

☆ *Hot water from geysers, is used to heat homes and offices in Reykjavik, the capital of Iceland.*

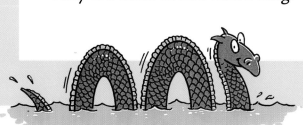

Glossary

chemical A substance that changes or can change things.

continent One of the seven large areas of land in the world.

core The center of Earth.

crust The outer layer of Earth.

energy The power to do work.

equator An imaginary line around the middle of Earth.

erode/erosion To wear away gradually.

extinct No longer alive or active.

force The power to make things happen.

fossil The remains of an animal or plant turned into stone.

glacier A huge, slow-moving sheet of ice.

gravity A **force** that pulls things toward each other.

habitat The place where an animal or plant usually lives.

lava Erupting **molten** rock and the same rock when hardened.

magma Hot or **molten** rock inside Earth.

mantle The thick layer of **molten** rock below Earth's **crust**.

orbit The path an object takes around a **planet** or star.

oxygen One of the gases in air. Animals breathe it to live.

planet A body in space moving around a star.

pressure The **force** of one thing pressing against another.

resource Something that can be useful.

temperature How hot or cold something is.

tide The regular rising and falling of the sea.

trench A very deep ditch.

valley The lower land between hills or mountains.

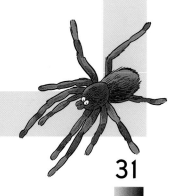

Index

www.two-canpublishing.com

Published in the United States and Canada by
Two-Can Publishing LLC
234 Nassau Street
Princeton, NJ 08542
in arrangement with
C.D. Stampley Enterprises, Inc.

© 2001, 1997 Two-Can Publishing
For information on Two-Can books and multimedia, call 1-609-921-6700, fax 1-609-921-3349, or visit our Web site at http://www.two-canpublishing.com

Text: Nicola Baxter
Consultant: Keith Lye
Watercolor artwork: Stuart Trotter
Computer artwork: D. Oliver
Commissioned photography: Steve Gorton
Photo Research: Dipika Palmer-Jenkins
Editorial Director: Jane Wilsher
Art Director: Carole Orbell
Production Director: Lorraine Estelle
Project Manager: Eljay Yildirim
Editor: Deborah Kespert
Assistant Editors: Julia Hillyard, Claire Yude
Co-edition Editor: Leila Peerun

'Two-Can' is a trademark of Two-Can Publishing. Two-Can Publishing is a division of Zenith Entertainment Ltd, 43-45 Dorset Street, London W1H 4AB

hc   ISBN 1-58728-2194
sc   ISBN 1-58728-2135

hc   2 3 4 5 6 7 8 9 10 02
sc   1 2 3 4 5 6 7 8 9 10 02 01

Photographic credits: Britstock-IFA (AP Gary Brettnacher) p25tr; Bruce Coleman Ltd (Jens Rydell) p7c, (Steven Kaufman) p8tr, (Gerald Cubitt) p24-25c; Eye Ubiquitous (Julia Waterlow) p23tr; Steve Gorton p7br, p28; Robert Harding p11r; Hutchison Library (Pern) p24bl; Pictor p13c, p19tr; Planet Earth Pictures p18-19c; Rex Features p10-11c; Tony Stone Images front cover, p10b, p15tr, p16b, p17r, p22-23c, p27b, p29tr; Telegraph Colour Library p20-21bc; Zefa p4bl, p9, p12r, p13tl, p14-15c, p17tl, p21tr, p21cr, p22cl, p26-27c.

Printed in Hong Kong